PASSIONS AND ANCIENT DAYS

OTHER BOOKS BY THE TRANSLATORS

Edmund Keeley

THE LIBATION

SIX POETS OF MODERN GREECE
with Philip Sherrard

THE GOLD-HATTED LOVER

VASSILIS VASSILIKOS: THE PLANT, THE WELL,
THE ANGEL
with Mary Keeley

GEORGE SEFERIS: COLLECTED POEMS, 1924–1955
with Philip Sherrard

THE IMPOSTOR

George Savidis

FOR SEFERIS

C. P. CAVAFY: POEMS, 1886–1933

ANGELOS SIKELIANOS: LYRIC LIFE

THE EDITIONS OF CAVAFY (1891–1932)

K. G. KARIOTAKIS: THE COMPLETE POEMS

C. P. CAVAFY: UNPUBLISHED POEMS, 1882–
1923

C. P. CAVAFY

PASSIONS AND ANCIENT DAYS

NEW POEMS TRANSLATED AND INTRODUCED BY

EDMUND KEELEY AND GEORGE SAVIDIS

THE DIAL PRESS / NEW YORK

Library of Congress Catalog Card Number: 70-131176

Printed in the United States of America

First printing

Book design by Richard Gabriel Rummonds

IN MEMORIAM / ALEXANDER SINGOPOULOS

CONTENTS

C. P. Cavafy's mode of publishing—or not publishing—his poems
was as original in its way as the poetry itself became once he found his
mature voice. The implications of this mode help to explain why it was
not until some thirty years after his death that the poems included in the
selection offered here finally appeared in print to complete the known
corpus of Cavafy's work.

> By my postponing, and repostponing to publish, what a gain I have had!
> Think of . . . trash [written] at the age of 25, 26, 27, and 28, of Byzantine
> poems . . . and many others which would disgrace me now.
> What a gain!
> And all those poems written between [the age of] 19 and 22. What
> wretched trash![1]

This violent self-condemnation (in the form of self-congratulation),
jotted down by Cavafy at the age of forty-three, constitutes the most
explicit testimony we have to the aesthetic perfectionism that apparently
made the poet reluctant to offer his poems publicly in permanent form
throughout his life. But we find equally convincing testimony in the
record of his work, a record that includes poems amply revised,
emended, discarded, kept in limbo, resurrected, offered for private
distribution, even published in some restricted way, but never collected
by the poet himself into a permanent volume that could stand for
Cavafy's own public image of his voice. Except for contributions to
periodicals and annuals, his poems were never really published at all in
the ordinary sense. He considered his poetic career to have begun
in 1891, though we know that he wrote copiously during the decade
before that, but between 1891 and 1904 he published only six poems
out of the 180-odd that he wrote or rewrote during this period, the
"publication" consisting of broadsheets or pamphlets printed on order
for distribution exclusively to his few friends and relatives.[2] In 1904,

at the age of forty-one, he collected fourteen poems in a privately printed pamphlet issued in one hundred copies as a sort of free sampler for those who might care to try his poetry. A second equally private and limited edition followed in 1910, increasing the sample to twenty-one poems out of the 220-odd that he had written by that date.[3] During the same year Cavafy devised a new system for distributing the latest installments of his life-long "work in progress" (as George Seferis has called it). Apparently distrusting the pamphlet method, which was too rigid to allow progressive revision of the text or the elimination of poems from the corpus, Cavafy developed a variation on the earlier broadsheet method which permitted both flexibility and the shaping of something like a volume: whenever a poem appeared in a periodical, the poet would order a set of off-prints primarily for distribution to the select few whom he considered his serious audience, or he would distribute broadsheets in advance of publication, and he would then gather the remnant of these "printings" into folders, with each new off-print or broadsheet clipped to the last and the title of the latest poem added by hand to a list of the contents. Though Cavafy never stopped offering single broadsheets to his closest friends, the distribution of these eccentric folders, kept always up to date, became the principal mode for promulgating his work.

By 1917, when the single clip in each folder could no longer bear the load of further broadsheets, Cavafy withdrew some of the earliest poems and had them sewn into booklets that were intended to accompany the ever-expanding folders, now given new life.[4] This process was repeated several times, so that at the poet's death in 1933, his "work in progress," still privately circulated, consisted of two sewn booklets containing a total of sixty-eight poems arranged thematically, and a folder of sixty-nine more recent poems arranged in order of first publication.[5] At no point during his lifetime did Cavafy offer a volume of his work for sale, and though his death was far from sudden, he left no definite instructions for the publication of a collected edition of his poems. The first such edition appeared two years after his death, sumptuously published by his heir, Alexander Singopoulos.[6]

As this history suggests, Cavafy maintained, along with an uncommon aesthetic asceticism, a strong sense of the tentative about his work throughout his fifty years as a poet. Although he faithfully recorded the birthdate and title of each newborn poem in a special catalogue of his work that he kept between 1891 and 1925,[7] he never considered a poem finished until he actually saw it in print, and even then it was subject to possible emendation or rejection (especially in the years before 1901). At the same time, a poem retained in manuscript form among his papers was always open to revision and ultimate publication. The poem "In Church," for example, was first written in 1892, revised in 1901, revised again in 1906, and finally published in 1912, to end a twenty-year period of trial. "If Dead Indeed" had an even longer gestation: from a first version in 1897 to publication in 1920. And among Cavafy's notes we find evidence that he returned regularly to his papers to dig out an early poem or an incomplete draft that might become the basis for publishable work. "A very old poem: can anything be made out of this?" he asks himself in a marginal comment on one of the unpublished poems not included here. We also find evidence, among the titles in his catalogue, of poems that were destroyed completely, particularly during his early years.

Most of the seventy-five so-called new poems from which our selection is taken apparently constituted that remnant of possibly redeemable work that Cavafy retained among his papers, presumably for ultimate revision and publication or as a source for new work. The fact is that any one of these unpublished poems could have gone the way of others that were destroyed; their having been preserved would seem to indicate a definite interest on Cavafy's part (as would the label "Not for publication, but may remain here" that the poet attached to a number of them). It is also a fact that some of those preserved—and we would include among these all that we offer here—are obviously good poems. Why, then, were these previously unpublished poems not incorporated into the collected edition of Cavafy that appeared two years after his death? The answer is that since Cavafy himself had not prepared them for publication, his heir felt that he had to honor the poet's tacit wishes in this regard by conveniently "forgetting" that there were unpublished poems in his possession. Also, at the time Singopoulos prepared the posthumous collected edition, Cavafy had a very limited reputation outside the Greek-speaking world, and his reputation in Greece and Egypt was hardly firm. This gave added strength to Singopoulos' impulse, since the inclusion of poems Cavafy himself had not chosen to publish in any form—some of which were clearly inferior to anything included in the printed canon—could serve to diminish the image of the poet he hoped to promote. Singopoulos, constantly protective, did not give anyone access to the Cavafy papers until after the Second World War, and even then the access he allowed was strictly controlled, so that no more than thirteen unpublished poems came to light between 1948 and 1963, when the first definitive edition of Cavafy's works was commissioned in connection with the centenary of his birth. At this time Singopoulos permitted the designated editor of Cavafy's poems, George Savidis, full access to the papers, and an additional sixty-two unpublished poems were thus brought to light, for ultimate publication in a scholarly edition of the new poems which appeared in Athens in 1968.[8]

Given the excellence of some of the new poems, one can't help wondering why Cavafy himself chose not to print them. Several answers suggest themselves. It is possible that some of the poems were regarded by Cavafy as thoroughly printable but were not published in any form for reasons other than their literary quality, for example, their being too personal, or too explicitly sexual, or too progressive for the taste of his particular community of readers ("Strengthening the Spirit," "Hidden Things," "Half an Hour," and "The Bandaged Shoulder" might well have been so regarded). It is also possible that several of the poems were considered by him to be good poems that were still in need of a final, final revision. In the case of some, his estimate of the poem's quality may simply have been too severe. That he was, in our view, generally correct in his judgement can be surmised from our having limited this selection to those twenty-one poems out of the sixty-two that we felt could stand beside the poems he chose to print during his maturity. We considered the remaining poems clearly inferior work, with the exception of a few that simply did not come over adequately into English and two that had to be excluded from our selection because their essential linguistic preoccupations were beyond translation (i.e., "Parthen" and "Coins"). A number of the new poems struck us as hardly more than early exercises with a certain value for the literary biographer but of small artistic merit. Still, we feel without hesitation that the best of the sixty-two re-covered during the past decade have the same claim to attention that the majority of the collected poems have. Their addition to the Cavafy corpus not only broadens our view of the poet—sometimes in startling ways—but provides us with new moments of the same insight and sensitivity that we find in the collected edition.

In an anonymous commentary on his work, Cavafy divided his printed poems into three major categories: the historical, the philosophical, and the erotic.[9] The new poems can also be seen to fall into the same categories, with the erotic and the historical the dominant modes, as our title suggests.[10] "Strengthening the Spirit" and "Hidden Things," though touching on the passions, are primarily "philosophical" poems, as is also true of "The Rest I Will Tell to Those Down in Hades," despite its historical façade. Of the three categories, the new historical poems are those that seem most typical of Cavafy; each reveals some analogy in theme or method to familiar historical poems among the collected works. We can perhaps see these new poems most clearly in the context of the old by examining some of the analogies. The first poem in this category, "Julian at the Mysteries," can be related directly to the group of six poems about Julian the Apostate that Cavafy published during the last decade of his life. Though the new poem antedates the earliest of this group by twenty-seven years, it is in very much the same mood. Julian is portrayed as a foolish figure, too easily awed by false gods, quite out of tune with his times, and with no trace of the romantic coloring that other late nineteenth-century writers (such as Ibsen and Cleon Rangavis) gave to his reactionary-revolutionary posture. As in the later poems, Cavafy here speaks from the perspective of those Christians contemporary with Julian who saw in him not a rebellious hero but a prudish and ridiculous anachronism bent on destroying their "delectable and absolutely elegant" life, as the poet puts it in "Julian and the Citizens of Antioch" (1926).[11] The principal difference is that in the early poem the Christianity which Julian repudiates comes over less as a way of life and more as an expression of religious conviction, in keeping with the persuasion of several other of Cavafy's early poems.[12]

The analogue in the case of "King Claudius" is one of method rather than subject. In fact, the subject is so far beyond the normal boundaries of Cavafy's world that one suspects the eccentricity of it may have been the principal reason the poet hesitated to include it among his printed poems, though it is obviously one of the more interesting of those he retained in his papers. The method of the poem, on the other hand, is entirely characteristic: an inverted rendering of the standard or expected response to some significant moment in history, the perspective that of someone viewing the action from a certain distance and with a degree of detachment. Several of Cavafy's poems in the Julian and Antony cycles are cases in point. Here the irony achieved by the "outsider's" perspective has a double edge. The voice of the poem is both that of the poet and that of an observer who "sees" the action as most people outside the court might have seen it: a kind of bourgeois view of events at Elsinore. At the same time, this bourgeois view, all suspicion and cynicism, comes in for its own touch of satire when we set it against the heroic world of Shakespeare that the poet introduces at the start and that remains implicit throughout the poem. The two faces of the poet's irony are not brought as clearly into focus in this poem as they are in Cavafy's best work—for example, in "Waiting for the Barbarians" (1904)—but the very ambiguity of the perspective is one element that keeps the narrative alive to the end of what is the poet's longest short story in verse.

"When the Watchman Saw the Light" is another poem that makes use of irony to provide a new slant on a significant moment in history. The great event is again viewed from the perspective of an average observer, and again the tone is one of political cynicism: as Fortinbras is seen to be in collusion with Horatio to gain easy access to the Danish throne, so the great King Agamemnon, about to return triumphantly from Troy to the Argive throne, is seen to be just another of your dispensable rulers with high-sounding titles who can be replaced at a moment's notice by someone equally dispensable, much as Octavius replaces Antony in the collected poem "In a Township of Asia Minor" (1926). The poet also plays with the kind of dramatic irony that characterizes "King Claudius" and so many of his poems that rely to some extent on the reader's foreknowledge of the historical context in question. In this instance, substance is given to the speaker's cynicism by what we know will be the fate of Agamemnon and his ancient house all too soon after his triumphant return. One is again reminded of the Antony cycle, most notably "Alexandrian Kings" (1912), which uses a similar technique to dramatize a related political insight.

Most of the remaining historical poems can be seen to offer new approaches to one of Cavafy's major preoccupations in the collected poems: the character of hellenism. As we know from the collected poems, Cavafy's view of hellenism was brilliantly complex. E. M. Forster was the first to suggest the dimensions of this complexity:

> [Cavafy] was a loyal Greek, but Greece for him was not territorial. It was rather the influence that has flowed from his race this way and that through the ages, and that (since Alexander the Great) has never disdained to mix with barbarism, has indeed desired to mix; the influence that made Byzantium a secular achievement. Racial purity bored him, so did political idealism . . . The civilization he respected was a bastardy in which the Greek strain prevailed, and into which, age after age, outsiders would push, to modify and be modified.[13]

The one dimension of Cavafy's hellenism that seems to elude Forster is that which is implicit in the new poem "Poseidonians": an almost mystical belief, at times, that to be Greek is the closest one can come to being godly on this earth, and to lose that quality is a kind of fall from paradise. It is the view expressed in the last stanza of "Epitaph of Antiochos King of Kommagênê" (1923):

> He had that superlative virtue: hellenism—
> mankind has no quality more valuable;
> anything beyond that belongs to the gods.

In "Poseidonians" we find a community of Greeks on the Tyrrhenian Gulf who have experienced such a fall from paradise on earth. After many centuries of mingling with Latins and other foreigners, the only Greek experience left to them is an annual festival with customs and a language they hardly understand, and the effect of the festival is simply to remind them each year of how completely they have lost that greatest of all things: the Hellenic way of life.

"Return from Greece" is a new poem that makes quite explicit the generous side of Cavafy's hellenism by dramatizing positively that sense of alienation from the Hellenic way of life that Greeks living in communities outside the mainland—Alexandria not least of all—must have felt on returning from a visit to the source. In this poem, the sense of alienation, of possessing affections and emotions "that hellenism sometimes finds strange," is not a cause for despair or shame: to be truly Greek is to accept the foreign influence without illusion or affectation—in fact, to honor fully the blood of Syria and Egypt that has mixed with the blood of Greece. The only cause for shame is to affect a hellenism that one doesn't really have, as in the "certain minor kings" of this poem, or in the Prince from Western Libya of the collected poems.

"Exiles" and "Theophilos Palaiologos" illustrate still different aspects of Cavafian hellenism. In the former we see a group of political exiles from the mainland attempting to create a plausible Greek world in the "wonderful" city of Alexandria, where they manage to survive on excursions, a bit of study, some talk of religion and literature, almost as they might at home. But what really keeps them alive during this "not unpleasant" stay abroad is their hope of an imminent return to the mother country, a hope that depends on friends moving to overthrow the Emperor Basil, who, history tells us, succeeded in never being overthrown at all. In "Theophilos Palaiologos" Cavafy offers us the only direct comment in his work on the fall of Constantinople (except for the folk-song incorporated into the highly original "Parthen," mentioned above). Typically, he approaches this decisive moment in history not from the perspective of the principal actor in it—the last of the emperors, Constantine Palaiologos—but from that of an intellectual in the Emperor's court, a lesser-known relative who is in a position to see and understand the full meaning of the event. What Theophilos Palaiologos sees, in effect, is the death of hellenism, and this inspires the despair of his words "I would rather die than live." It also inspires the poet to give us his definition of the dominant mood in

Greek history, what George Seferis has called "o kaimos tis romio-
sinis": the surfeit of sorrow and injustice that seems to have been the
fate of the Greek people from the beginning to the present day.

The two new historical poems that remain, "The End of Antony"
and "Simeon," offer obvious analogies to poems familiar to us from
the collected works. The former adds a new point of view to the
cycle of five published poems about Antony and Cleopatra; in fact,
there is no other poem in the Cavafy corpus that treats a Roman
subject with this degree of sympathy. Here, instead of diminishing
Antony, as in "Alexandrian Kings," or admonishing him to rise up
with courage so as to be worthy of the Greek city he has known so
well, as in "The God Abandons Antony" (1911), we find Cavafy
portraying Antony almost as though he were a Greek—a Demetrios
Soter or a Manuel Komnenos or the Spartan mother of King Kleo-
menes—ready to face defeat with the knowledge of who he really is,
and with full pride in this knowledge. "Simeon," perhaps the best
dramatic monologue that Cavafy ever wrote, epitomizes the
mature poet in both method and theme. Like the one or two other
fully developed dramatic monologues in the collected poems (such as
"Philhellene," 1912), Cavafy here makes subtle use of the listener in the
poem to create a sense of heightened narration on the speaker's part.
The poet also succeeds in conveying a realistic attitude toward his
material through a speaker who reveals himself to be both engaged in
the things of this world and compassionate toward things beyond it.
The perspective is again that of the outsider, and the kind of outsider
who appealed to Cavafy: the non-Christian caught up for a moment
by a Christian ritual or mystery that he cannot ever fully share. The
principal analogue in the collected poems is "Myres: Alexandria:
A. D. 340" (1929), a moving evocation of a related theme, though a
less sophisticated monologue. The new poem is so obviously a product
of mature craftsmanship that it is hard to find any hint in the text as
to why Cavafy chose not to print it.

The three poems that we have characterized as "philosophical" cannot be so easily related to the collected poems; each is in its way unique. "Strengthening the Spirit," for example, presents a point of view so modern, so far ahead of the times in which it was written (the turn of the century), that it is not difficult to see why Cavafy might have feared that it would subject him to critical attack if it were distributed in Alexandria during his lifetime. For a poet to declare that the road to virtue lies in living beyond the established norm, or to suggest that there is room for the destructive act, could be a hazardous position to take in the Greek world even today. On the other hand, it would be a mistake to see Cavafy as a pure prophet of the New Left; he tells us that some laws must be honored, and that only half the house must be pulled down. And two aspects of the poem are relatively conventional within the Cavafian context: the didactic tone of it, and the role assigned to pleasure, which clearly anticipates the "Ithaka" theme that appears in his work a few years later.

"Hidden Things" must be among the more overtly personal poems that Cavafy wrote, and it is probably the most revealing about his torment as an artist—about his long incapacity to tell things exactly the way they were. The poem would seem to explain why a number of his most honest and realistic love poems ("The Bandaged Shoulder," "Half an Hour," "At the Theatre," "On the Stairs") remained among his papers; and it also suggests why these "hidden things" now seem to speak with particular truthfulness. The language of the poem (in the original) is as direct and unpretentious as any the poet used. Another unusual element in it is the concluding reference to "a more perfect society," the only direct evidence of this kind of speculation on Cavafy's part that we find in his poetic work, printed or otherwise.

The last of the "philosophical" poems, "The Rest I Will Tell to Those Down in Hades," carries the message of "Hidden Things" a step forward. The proconsul speaks much as the poet of the earlier poem did: in Hades the obstacles that keep us from speaking openly will be gone, the locked-in secrets that give us our daily anxiety will be revealed. In this sense Hades becomes the proconsul's substitute for the perfect society of the earlier poem. And that is where the concluding irony lies, the touch of cynical truth that the sophist offers us for a commentary on the proconsul's view of "hidden things": if the afterlife is to be our perfect society where we can reveal all freely and clearly, how can we be certain that we'll find anyone there who will bother to listen to matters that belong so much to the world we left behind?

"September, 1903," the earliest of the nine poems belonging to the file called "Passions," establishes a major theme of the erotic group in its opening line: "At least let me now deceive myself with illusions." Throughout these poems we find a dramatization of the vital tensions between illusion and reality, or imagination and actuality, in erotic experience. At moments—as in this poem—illusion is seen as a palliative for the loss of a reality that was almost achieved but remained ultimately unrealized: a reality that is seen to be worth achieving. At other moments, the reality of love seems to reside not so much in palpable experience as in images that the mind is stimulated to construct by an erotic impulse. In "At the Theatre," for example, the theatrical performance which most enraptures the speaker is that of his own imagination in "picturing" the object of his attention "the way they'd talked about [him] that same afternoon." Again, in "The Photograph," the speaker dismisses the crude (and probably heterosexual) reality depicted in the obscene photograph in order to preserve, for the purposes of his art, a dreamlike image of the figure shown there, a figure "shaped for and dedicated to Hellenic love." We find a more extreme variation on the same theme in "On Hearing of Love," where the speaker actually designates real and tangible loves as lesser than those the imagination creates. But the most persuasive dramatization of the theme is that of "Half an Hour," one of the most memorable erotic poems that Cavafy wrote in any year. The poem opens with an expression of the speaker's regret over his failure to realize a tangible reality, then moves on to a crucial qualification:

> . . . But we who serve Art,
> sometimes by intensity of mind and of course only
> for a short time, are able to create pleasure
> which seems almost tangible.
> That's how in the bar yesterday—
> with the help of compassionate alcohol—
> I had half an hour that was totally erotic.

The word "totally" introduces complex implications: though the experience fashioned by the imagination is something less than tangible (as "almost" would indicate), it is nevertheless total, even perfect (the Greek permits either rendering). One is led to wonder whether the speaker, for all his regret, would make the same claim for any actual experience that he may have had. He tells us, in effect, that the artist, by intensity of mind, can know that which the lover will probably never know, however tangible and however realized his erotic commitment. At the same time, he suggests that the imagination must always be rooted in a physical reality. The poem concludes with the implication that however total or perfect the imagined experience in this instance, it still required an almost tangible consciousness of the loved one's physical presence to be as real as it was:

> for all the imagination, for all the magic alcohol,
> I needed to see your lips as well,
> I needed your body to be near.

The physical presence must be there, but when the poet comes to recreate the experience in his verse (as compelling an impulse here as in the collected poems), the recreation is never very precise, never clearly personalized: hair, lips, and eyes without color or particularity (as in "December, 1903") or simply a sensation of physical presence, of "body sensing body" (as in "On the Stairs"). The settings in these poems, though typical of Cavafy, also remain generalized—an undefined bar or house of illicit pleasure or theatre—with little of the detail that we find in some of the more familiar of his collected erotic poems (for instance, "The Afternoon Sun," 1919, and "To Remain," 1919). Again, it would seem that the poet's dreaming imagination must not be cluttered by too much actuality, as it must not be cluttered by too much history in the collected "Kaisarion" (1918):

> . . . History has preserved
> only a few lines about you,
> and so I pictured you with greater freedom in my mind.

At the same time, the imagination appears most alive when it is aroused by certain precise and sometimes palpable stimulants; in the best of the new erotic poems, these serve to create that sense of the actual which makes the passions depicted convincing. In "Half an Hour" it is "compassionate alcohol" (the Greek literally means "alcoholism"); in "On the Stairs" it is a single quick glance from "tired and suspect eyes"; in "At the Theatre" it is the appearance of "discriminating dress" in conjunction with "tired beauty" and "tired youth"; and in "The Bandaged Shoulder," perhaps the most avant-garde of this group in its rawness, it is the bloody rag that the speaker holds to his lips. These are the details that bring home a sense of reality, of felt intensity. The context of the new poems almost always projects an eroticism that depends on some degree of artifice, on at least a partial—if sometimes exquisitely painful—exorcism in verse, on the recreating imagination working at one remove from precision and actuality: an eroticism that is realized by "intensity of mind" above all else because the physical reality remains too vague or too unrealized to satisfy totally; yet that which stimulates the imagination is the occasional concrete detail, sometimes more direct and tangible than anything equivalent that appears in the collected works.

The language of these poems also serves to reinforce the sense of felt experience in them. Most of the poems included in this selection follow the pattern of the collected poems in offering a demotic qualified by purist elements, but the best of the erotic poems are as close to the *spoken* idiom as any poetry written by the modern masters since Cavafy. In "Half an Hour" and "The Bandaged Shoulder," for example, the diction is strictly demotic, and the only trace of purist that remains is an occasional ending. It is also apparent from the most recent of these poems, as from many of the collected poems, that in his mature years Cavafy achieved an increasingly colloquial tone in his erotic poetry (and to a degree in all his poetry) by employing an increasingly non-traditional diction and a choice of rhythms close to those of everyday speech, with none of the literary or sentimental overtones that we sometimes hear in his early verse (and that color, for example, "September, 1903" and "December, 1903" to a degree). No translation can give an accurate image of the poet's development in this regard, or of the particular quality of Cavafy's Greek at any stage in his evolution, which, in these poems, covers a period of more than twenty-five years. Obviously no translation can exploit, or even successfully imitate, the particular linguistic resources that Cavafy was able to tap in creating the tone of individual poems. What this translation attempts to capture, with as little injury as possible, is the special sensibility that pervades Cavafy's work and that should show through any rendering: what W. H. Auden has called his "unique tone of voice."[14] In courting this tone, we have looked for a contemporary idiom that is neither so special as to seem precious nor so current as to seem temporary: what we hope is an idom close in spirit to that which Cavafy was striving for in his maturest verse.

Athens, 1970.   E.K. & G.P.S.

THE POEMS

Ο ΙΟΥΛΙΑΝΟΣ ΕΝ ΤΟΙΣ ΜΥΣΤΗΡΙΟΙΣ

Πλὴν σὰν εὑρέθηκε μέσα στὸ σκότος,
μέσα στῆς γῆς τὰ φοβερὰ τὰ βάθη,
συντροφευμένος μ' Ἕλληνας ἀθέους,
κ' εἶδε μὲ δόξες καὶ μεγάλα φῶτα
νὰ βγαίνουν ἄϋλες μορφὲς ἐμπρός του,
φοβήθηκε γιὰ μιὰ στιγμὴν ὁ νέος,
κ' ἕνα ἔνστικτον τῶν εὐσεβῶν του χρόνων
ἐπέστρεψε, κ' ἔκαμε τὸν σταυρό του.
Ἀμέσως οἱ Μορφὲς ἀφανισθῆκαν·
οἱ δόξες χάθηκαν — σβύσαν τὰ φῶτα.
Οἱ Ἕλληνες ἐκρυφοκυτταχθῆκαν.
Κι ὁ νέος εἶπεν· «Εἴδατε τὸ θαῦμα;
Ἀγαπητοί μου σύντροφοι, φοβοῦμαι.
Φοβοῦμαι, φίλοι μου, θέλω νὰ φύγω.
Δὲν βλέπετε πῶς χάθηκαν ἀμέσως
οἱ δαίμονες σὰν μ' εἴδανε νὰ κάνω
τὸ σχῆμα τοῦ σταυροῦ τὸ ἁγιασμένο;»
Οἱ Ἕλληνες ἐκάγχασαν μεγάλα·
«Ντροπή, ντροπὴ νὰ λὲς αὐτὰ τὰ λόγια
σὲ μᾶς τοὺς σοφιστὰς καὶ φιλοσόφους.
Τέτοια σὰν θὲς εἰς τὸν Νικομηδείας
καὶ στοὺς παπάδες του μπορεῖς νὰ λές.
Τῆς ἔνδοξης Ἑλλάδος μας ἐμπρός σου
οἱ μεγαλύτεροι θεοὶ φανῆκαν.
Κι ἂν φύγανε νὰ μὴ νομίζεις διόλου

JULIAN AT THE MYSTERIES

But when he found himself in darkness,
in the earth's awful depths,
in the company of godless Greeks,
and with halos and a great show of light
bodiless figures appeared before him,
the young man suddenly became afraid:
an instinct of his pious years returned
and he crossed himself.
The Figures disappeared at once;
the halos vanished, the lights went out.
The Greeks glanced at each other.
The young man said: "Did you see the miracle?
My dear companions, I'm afraid.
I'm afraid, my friends. I want to leave.
Didn't you see how the demons disappeared
the second they saw me make the holy sign of the cross?"
The Greeks chortled loudly:
"Shame, shame on you to talk that way
to us sophists and philosophers.
If you want to say things like that
go say them to the Bishop of Nicomedia
and his priests. The greatest gods
of our glorious Greece appeared before you.
And if they left do not think for a minute

πού φοβηθῆκαν μιὰ χειρονομία.
Μονάχα σὰν σὲ εἴδανε νὰ κάνεις
τὸ ποταπότατον, ἀγροῖκον σχῆμα
συχάθηκεν ἡ εὐγενής των φύσις
καὶ φύγανε καὶ σὲ περιφρονῆσαν ».
Ἔτσι τὸν εἴπανε, κι ἀπὸ τὸν φόβο
τὸν ἱερὸν καὶ τὸν εὐλογημένον
συνῆλθεν ὁ ἀνόητος, κ' ἐπείσθη
μὲ τῶν Ἑλλήνων τ' ἄθεα τὰ λόγια.

1896

that they were frightened by a gesture.
It was just that when they saw you
making that most vile and crude sign,   5
their noble nature was disgusted
and they left you in contempt."
This they said to him, and the fool
recovered from his holy and blessed fear,
convinced by the godless words of the Greeks.

Ο ΒΑΣΙΛΕΥΣ ΚΛΑΥΔΙΟΣ

Σὲ μέρη μακρυνὰ ὁ νοῦς μου πιαίνει.
Στοὺς δρόμους περπατῶ τῆς Ἐλσινόρης,
γυρίζω στὲς πλατεῖες, καὶ θυμοῦμαι
τὴν θλιβερώτατη τὴν ἱστορία,
τὸν ἄτυχον ἐκεῖνον βασιλέα,
ποὺ τὸν ἐσκότωσεν ὁ ἀνεψιός του
γιὰ κάτ' ἰδανικές του ὑποψίες.

Σ' ὅλα τὰ σπίτια τῶν πτωχῶν ἀνθρώπων
κρυφὰ (γιατὶ τὸν Φορτιμπρᾶς φοβοῦνταν)
τὸν ἔκλαψαν. Φιλήσυχος καὶ πρᾶος
ἦταν· καὶ τὴν εἰρήνην ἀγαποῦσε
(πολλὰ ὁ τόπος εἶχεν ὑποφέρει
ἀπὸ τοῦ προκατόχου του τὲς μάχες).
Εὐγενικὰ ἐφέρνονταν πρὸς ὅλους,
μεγάλους καὶ μικρούς. Αὐθαιρεσίες
ἐχθρεύονταν, καὶ συμβουλὲς ζητοῦσε
στοῦ βασιλείου τὲς ὑποθέσεις πάντα
ἀπὸ ἀνθρώπους σοβαροὺς κ' ἐμπείρους.

Γιατί τὸν σκότωσεν ὁ ἀνεψιός του
μὲ θετικότητα ποτὲ δὲν εἶπαν.
Τὸν ὑπωπτεύετο γιὰ ἕναν φόνο.
Τῆς ὑποψίας του ἡ βάσις ἦταν

KING CLAUDIUS

My mind moves to distant places.
I'm walking the streets of Elsinore,
through its squares, and I recall
the very sad story—
that unfortunate king
killed by his nephew
because of some fanciful suspicions.

In all the homes of the poor people
secretly (because they were afraid of Fortinbras)
he was mourned. A quiet, gentle man;
a man who loved peace
(his country had suffered much
from the wars of his predecessor).
He behaved graciously toward everyone,
the humble and the great alike.
Never high-handed, he always sought advice
in the kingdom's affairs
from serious and experienced persons.

Just why his nephew killed him
was never satisfactorily explained.
The prince suspected him of murder;
and the basis of his suspicion was this:

πού σάν μιά νύχτα περπατοῦσε ἐπάνω
σ' ἕναν ἀπ' τοὺς ἀρχαίους προμαχῶνας,
ἐθάρρεψε πὼς εἶδεν ἕνα φάσμα
καὶ μὲ τὸ φάσμα ἔκαμ' ὁμιλία.
Καὶ τάχα κάποιες ἔμαθ' ἀπ' τὸ φάσμα
κατηγορίες γιὰ τὸν βασιλέα.

Θὰ ἦταν ἔξαψις τῆς φαντασίας
βεβαίως καὶ τῶν ὀφθαλμῶν ἀπάτη.
(Ὁ πρίγκηψ ἦταν νευρικὸς εἰς ἄκρον.
Σὰν σπούδαζε στὸ Βίττεμπεργκ τὸν εἶχαν
γιὰ μανιακὸ πολλοὶ συμμαθηταί του).

Ὀλίγες μέρες ἔπειτα ἐπῆγεν
εἰς τῆς μητέρας του νὰ ὁμιλήσουν
γιὰ μερικὰ οἰκογενειακά των. Κ' αἴφνης
ἐκεῖ ποὺ ὁμιλοῦσε παρεφέρθη
κι ἄρχισε νὰ βοᾶ, νὰ ξεφωνίζει
πὼς φάνηκε τὸ φάσμα ἐμπροστά του.
Πλὴν τίποτ' ἡ μητέρα του δὲν εἶδε.

Καὶ τὴν ἰδία μέρα ἕναν γέρον
ἄρχοντα σκότωσε χωρὶς αἰτία.
Καθὼς ἐπρόκειτο νὰ πάγει ὁ πρίγκηψ
εἰς τὴν Ἀγγλία σὲ μιὰ δύο ἡμέρες,
ὁ βασιλεὺς ἐπέσπευσ' ἄρον, ἄρον
τὸν πηγαιμό του γιὰ νὰ τὸν γλυτώσει.
Πλὴν τόσο ἀγανάκτησεν ὁ κόσμος

walking one night along an ancient battlement
he thought he saw a ghost
and with this ghost had a talk;
what he heard from the ghost supposedly
were certain accusations made against the king.

It must have been a fit of fancy
and an optical illusion
(the prince was nervous in the extreme;
while studying at Wittenberg
many of his fellow students thought him a maniac).

A few days later he went
to his mother's chambers to discuss
some family affairs. And suddenly,
while he was talking, he lost his self-control
and started shouting, screaming,
that the ghost was there in front of him.
But his mother saw nothing at all.

And that same day, for no apparent reason,
he killed an old gentleman of the court.
Since the prince was due to sail for England
in a day or two,
the king hustled him off posthaste
in order to save him.
But the people were so outraged

για την φρικτότατη δολοφονία,
που εσηκώθηκαν επαναστάται
και γύρευαν του παλατιού τες πόρτες
να σπάσουν με τον υιό του σκοτωμένου
τον άρχοντα Λαέρτη (έναν νέον
ανδρείο, και φιλόδοξον επίσης·
στην ταραχή «Ο Βασιλεύς Λαέρτης
ζήτω!» εφώναξαν κάποιοι του φίλοι).

Σαν έπειτα ησύχασεν ο τόπος
κι ο βασιλεύς ξαπλώθηκε στον τάφο
από τον ανεψιό του σκοτωμένος
(ο πρίγκηψ στην Αγγλία δεν επήγε·
στον δρόμο ξέφυγεν από το πλοίο),
ένας Οράτιος βγήκε στην μέση
κ' εγύρεψε με κάτι εξιστορήσεις
τον πρίγκηπα να δικαιολογήσει.
Είπε πως το ταξείδι της Αγγλίας
ήταν επιβουλή κρυφή, κ' εδόθη
διαταγή εκεί να τον σκοτώσουν.
(Αυτό όμως καθαρά δεν απεδείχθη).
Είπε και για κρασί φαρμακευμένο,
φαρμακευμένο απ' τον βασιλέα.
Τό'πε, είν' αλήθεια, κι ο Λαέρτης τούτο.
Πλην δεν εψεύσθη; πλην δεν απατήθη;

by the monstrous murder
that rebels rose up
and tried to storm the palace gates,
led by the dead man's son,
the noble lord Laertes
(a brave young man, and also ambitious;
in the confusion, some of his friends called out:
"Long live King Laertes!").

Some time later, once the kingdom had calmed down
and the king lay resting in his grave,
killed by his nephew
(the prince never went to England;
he escaped from the ship on his way there),
a certain Horatio came forward
and tried to exonerate the prince
by telling some stories of his own.
He said that the voyage to England
had been a secret plot, and orders
had been given to kill the prince there
(but this was never clearly ascertained).
He also spoke of poisoned wine—
wine poisoned by the king.
It's true that Laertes spoke of this too.
But couldn't he have been lying?
Couldn't he have been mistaken?

Καὶ πότε τό'πε; Ὅταν πληγωμένος
ἐξέπνεε, κ' ἐγύριζεν ὁ νοῦς του,
καὶ φαίνονταν σὰν νὰ παραμιλοῦσε.
Ὅσο γιὰ τὰ φαρμακευμένα ὅπλα
κατόπι φάνηκε πὼς τὸ φαρμάκι
δὲν τό'βαλεν ὁ βασιλεὺς καθόλου,
μονάχος του τό'βαλεν ὁ Λαέρτης.
Ἀλλὰ ὁ Ὁράτιος εἰς τὴν ἀνάγκη
ἔβγαζε καὶ τὸ φάσμα μαρτυρία.
Τὸ φάσμα εἶπε τοῦτο, εἶπ' ἐκεῖνο!
Τὸ φάσμα ἔκαμεν αὐτὸ κ' ἐκεῖνο!

Γι' αὐτά, ἐνῶ τὸν ἄκουαν νὰ λέγει,
οἱ πιὸ πολλοὶ μὲς στὴν συνείδησί των
λυποῦνταν τὸν καλὸ τὸν βασιλέα
ποὺ μὲ φαντάσματα καὶ παραμύθια
ἄδικα τὸν ἐσκότωσαν, καὶ πῆγε.

Ὅμως ὁ Φορτιμπρᾶς, ποὺ ὠφελήθη
κι ἀπέκτησ' εὔκολα τὴν ἐξουσία,
κῦρος πολὺ καὶ προσοχὴ μεγάλη
ἔδιδεν εἰς τὰ λόγια τοῦ Ὁρατίου.

1899

And when did he speak of this?
While dying of his wounds, his mind reeling,
and seeming to talk deliriously.
As for the poisoned weapons,
it was shown later that the poisoning
had not been done by the king at all:
Laertes had done it himself.
But Horatio, whenever pressed,
would produce even the ghost as a witness:
the ghost said this and that,
the ghost did this and that!

Because of all this, though hearing him out,
most people in their hearts
pitied the poor king,
who, with all these ghosts and fairy tales,
was unjustly killed and disposed of.

Yet Fortinbras, who profited from it all
and so easily won the throne,
gave full attention and weight
to every word Horatio said.

OTAN O ΦΥΛΑΞ ΕΙΔΕ ΤΟ ΦΩΣ

Χειμῶνα, καλοκαῖρι κάθονταν στὴν στέγη
τῶν Ἀτρειδῶν κ' ἔβλεπ' ὁ Φύλαξ. Τώρα λέγει
εὐχάριστα. Μακρυὰ εἶδε φωτιὰ ν' ἀνάβει.
Καὶ χαίρεται· κι ὁ κόπος του ἐπίσης παύει.
Εἶναι ἐπίπονον καὶ νύκτα καὶ ἡμέρα,
στὴν ζέστη καὶ στὸ κρύο νὰ κυττάζεις πέρα
τὸ Ἀραχναῖον γιὰ φωτιά. Τώρα ἐφάνη
τὸ ἐπιθυμητὸν σημεῖον. Ὅταν φθάνει
ἡ εὐτυχία, δίδει πιὸ μικρὴ χαρὰ
ἀπ' ὅ,τι προσδοκᾶ κανείς. Πλὴν καθαρὰ
τοῦτο κερδήθηκε: γλυτώσαμ' ἀπ' ἐλπίδας
καὶ προσδοκίας. Πράγματα εἰς τοὺς Ἀτρείδας
πολλὰ θὰ γίνουνε. Χωρὶς νά 'ναι σοφὸς
κανεὶς εἰκάζει τοῦτο τώρα ποὺ τὸ φῶς
εἶδεν ὁ Φύλαξ. Ὅθεν μὴ ὑπερβολή.
Καλὸ τὸ φῶς· κι αὐτοὶ ποὺ ἔρχονται καλοί·
τὰ λόγια καὶ τὰ ἔργα των κι αὐτὰ καλά.
Καὶ ὅλα ἴσια νὰ εὐχόμεθα. Ἀλλὰ
τὸ Ἄργος ἠμπορεῖ χωρὶς Ἀτρείδας νὰ
κάμει. Τὰ σπίτια δὲν εἶναι παντοτεινά.
Πολλοὶ βεβαίως θὰ μιλήσουνε πολλά.
Ἡμεῖς ν' ἀκοῦμε. Ὅμως δὲν θὰ μᾶς γελᾶ
τὸ Ἀπαραίτητος, τὸ Μόνος, τὸ Μεγάλος.
Καὶ ἀπαραίτητος, καὶ μόνος, καὶ μεγάλος
ἀμέσως πάντα βρίσκεται κανένας ἄλλος.

1900

WHEN THE WATCHMAN SAW THE LIGHT

Winter, summer, the watchman sat there looking out
from the palace roof of the sons of Atreus.
Now he has good news to report. He's seen the fire light up
in the distance and he's glad: also, the drudgery is over.
It's hard to sit there night and day in heat and cold,
on the lookout for a fire to show
on the peak of Arachnaion.
Now the longed-for signal has appeared. When happiness comes
it brings less joy than one expected.
This much is clearly gained, however: we've rid ourselves
of hope and expectation. Many things will happen
to the sons of Atreus. No need to be wise
to guess this now the watchman has seen the light.
So let's not exaggerate.
The light is good; and those coming are good;
their words and their actions also good.
And let's hope all goes well.
But Argos can do without the sons of Atreus.
Ancient houses are not eternal.
Of course many people will have much to say.
We should listen. But we won't be deceived
by titles such as Indispensable, Unique, and Great.
Someone else indispensable and unique and great
can always be found at a moment's notice.

ΔΥΝΑΜΩΣΙΣ

Ὅποιος τὸ πνεῦμα του ποθεῖ νὰ δυναμώσει,
νὰ βγῆ ἀπ' τὸ σέβας κι ἀπὸ τὴν ὑποταγή.
Ἀπὸ τοὺς νόμους μερικοὺς θὰ τοὺς φυλάξει,
ἀλλὰ τὸ περισσότερο θὰ παραβαίνει
καὶ νόμους κ' ἔθιμα, κι ἀπ' τὴν παραδεγμένη
καὶ τὴν ἀνεπαρκοῦσα εὐθύτητα θὰ βγεῖ.
Ἀπὸ τὲς ἡδονὲς πολλὰ θὰ διδαχθεῖ.
Τὴν καταστρεπτικὴ δὲν θὰ φοβᾶται πρᾶξι·
τὸ σπίτι τὸ μισὸ πρέπει νὰ γκρεμισθεῖ.
Ἔτσι θ' ἀναπτυχθεῖ ἐνάρετα στὴν γνῶσι.

1903

STRENGTHENING THE SPIRIT

He who longs to strengthen his spirit
must go beyond obedience and respect.
He will continue to honor some laws
but he will mostly violate
both law and custom, and reach beyond
the established and deficient norm.
Pleasure will have much to teach him.
He will not be afraid of the destructive act;
one half of the house must be pulled down.
This way he will grow virtuously into knowledge.

Ο ΣΕΠΤΕΜΒΡΗΣ ΤΟΥ 1903

Τουλάχιστον μὲ πλάνες ἂς γελιοῦμαι τώρα·
τὴν ἄδεια τὴν ζωή μου νὰ μὴ νοιώθω.

Καὶ ἤμουνα τόσες φορὲς τόσο κοντά.
Καὶ πῶς παρέλυσα, καὶ πῶς δειλίασα·
γιατί νὰ μείνω μὲ κλειστὰ τὰ χείλη·
καὶ μέσα μου νὰ κλαίει ἡ ἄδεια μου ζωή,
καὶ νὰ μαυροφοροῦν οἱ ἐπιθυμίες μου.

Τόσες φορὲς τόσο κοντὰ νὰ εἶμαι
στὰ μάτια, καὶ στὰ χείλη τὰ ἐρωτικά,
στ᾽ ὀνειρεμένο, τὸ ἀγαπημένο σῶμα.
Τόσες φορὲς τόσο κοντὰ νὰ εἶμαι.

1904

At least let me now deceive myself with illusions
so as not to feel my empty life. ·

And yet I came so close so many times.
And yet how paralyzed I was, how cowardly;
why did I keep my lips sealed
while my empty life wept inside me,
my desires dressed in black ?

To have been so close so many times
to the eyes of love, the lips,
to the body dreamed of, loved.
So close so many times.

Ο ΔΕΚΕΜΒΡΗΣ ΤΟΥ 1903

20

Κι ἂν γιὰ τὸν ἔρωτά μου δὲν μπορῶ νὰ πῶ —
ἂν δὲν μιλῶ γιὰ τὰ μαλλιά σου, γιὰ τὰ χείλη, γιὰ τὰ μάτια·
ὅμως τὸ πρόσωπό σου ποὺ κρατῶ μὲς στὴν ψυχή μου,
ὁ ἦχος τῆς φωνῆς σου ποὺ κρατῶ μὲς στὸ μυαλό μου,
οἱ μέρες τοῦ Σεπτέμβρη ποὺ ἀνατέλλουν στὰ ὄνειρά μου,
τὲς λέξεις καὶ τὲς φράσεις μου πλάττουν καὶ χρωματίζουν
εἰς ὅποιο θέμα κι ἂν περνῶ, ὅποιαν ἰδέα κι ἂν λέγω.

1904

DECEMBER, 1903

And if I can't speak about my love—
if I don't talk about your hair, your lips, your eyes,
still your face that I keep inside my soul,
the sound of your voice that I keep inside my brain,
the days of September rising in my dreams,
give shape and color to my words, my sentences,
whatever theme I touch, whatever thought I utter.

ΣΤΕΣ ΣΚΑΛΕΣ

Τὴν ἄτιμη τὴν σκάλα σὰν κατέβαινα,
ἀπὸ τὴν πόρτα ἔμπαινες, καὶ μιὰ στιγμὴ
εἶδα τὸ ἄγνωστό σου πρόσωπο καὶ μὲ εἶδες.
Ἔπειτα κρύφθηκα νὰ μὴ μὲ ξαναδεῖς, καὶ σὺ
πέρασες γρήγορα, τὸ πρόσωπό σου κρύβοντας,
καὶ χώθηκες στὸ ἄτιμο τὸ σπίτι μέσα
ὅπου τὴν ἡδονὴ δὲν θά'βρες, καθὼς δὲν τὴν βρῆκα.

Κι ὅμως τὸν ἔρωτα ποὺ ἤθελες τὸν εἶχα νὰ στὸν δώσω·
τὸν ἔρωτα ποὺ ἤθελα — τὰ μάτια σου μὲ τό'παν
τὰ κουρασμένα καὶ ὕποπτα— εἶχες νὰ μὲ τὸν δώσεις.
Τὰ σώματά μας αἰσθανθῆκαν καὶ γυρεύονταν·
τὸ αἷμα καὶ τὸ δέρμα μας ἐνόησαν.

Ἀλλὰ κρυφθήκαμε κ' οἱ δυό μας ταραγμένοι.

1904

ON THE STAIRS

As I was going down the infamous stairs
you were coming through the door, and for a second
I saw your unfamiliar face and you saw me.
Then I hid myself so you wouldn't see me again,
and you hurried past me, hiding your face,
and slipped inside the infamous house
where you couldn't have found pleasure any more than I did.

And yet the love you were looking for, I had to give you;
the love I was looking for—so your tired, suspect eyes implied—
you had to give me.
Our bodies sensed and sought each other;
our blood and skin understood.

But we both hid ourselves, flustered.

ΣΤΟ ΘΕΑΤΡΟ

Βαρέθηκα νὰ βλέπω τὴν σκηνή,
καὶ σήκωσα τὰ μάτια μου στὰ θεωρεῖα.
Καὶ μέσα σ' ἕνα θεωρεῖο εἶδα σένα
μὲ τὴν παράξενη ἐμορφιά σου, καὶ τὰ διεφθαρμένα νειάτα.
Κι ἀμέσως γύρισαν στὸν νοῦ μου πίσω
ὅσα μὲ εἴπανε τὸ ἀπόγευμα γιὰ σένα,
κ' ἡ σκέψις καὶ τὸ σῶμα μου συγκινηθῆκαν.
Κ' ἐνῶ ἐκύτταζα γοητευμένος
τὴν κουρασμένη σου ἐμορφιά, τὰ κουρασμένα νειάτα,
τὸ ντύσιμό σου τὸ ἐκλεκτικό,
σὲ φανταζόμουν καὶ σὲ εἰκόνιζα,
καθὼς μὲ εἴπανε τὸ ἀπόγευμα γιὰ σένα.

1904

AT THE THEATRE

I got bored looking at the stage
and raised my eyes to the box circle.
In one of the boxes I saw you
with your strange beauty, your corrupt youth.
My thoughts turned back at once
to all I'd heard about you that afternoon;
my mind and body were aroused.
And as I gazed enthralled
at your tired beauty, your tired youth,
your discriminating dress,
in my imagination I kept picturing you
the way they'd talked about you that afternoon.

ΠΟΣΕΙΔΩΝΙΑΤΑΙ

Ποσειδωνιάταις τοῖς ἐν τῷ Τυρρηνικῷ κόλπῳ τὸ μὲν
ἐξ ἀρχῆς Ἕλλησιν οὖσιν ἐκβαρβαρῶσθαι Τυρρηνοῖς
ἢ Ρωμαίοις γεγονόσι καὶ τήν τε φωνὴν μεταβεβλη-
κέναι, τά τε πολλὰ τῶν ἐπιτηδευμάτων, ἄγειν δὲ μιάν
τινα αὐτοὺς τῶν ἑορτῶν τῶν Ἑλλήνων ἔτι καὶ νῦν,
ἐν ᾗ συνιόντες ἀναμιμνήσκονται τῶν ἀρχαίων ὀνομάτων
τε καὶ νομίμων, ἀπολοφυράμενοι πρὸς ἀλλήλους καὶ
δακρύσαντες ἀπέρχονται.

ΑΘΗΝΑΙΟΣ

Τὴν γλῶσσα τὴν ἑλληνικὴ οἱ Ποσειδωνιᾶται
ἐξέχασαν τόσους αἰῶνας ἀνακατευμένοι
μὲ Τυρρηνούς, καὶ μὲ Λατίνους, κι ἄλλους ξένους.
Τὸ μόνο ποὺ τοὺς ἔμενε προγονικὸ
ἦταν μιὰ ἑλληνικὴ γιορτή, μὲ τελετὲς ὡραῖες,
μὲ λύρες καὶ μὲ αὐλούς, μὲ ἀγῶνας καὶ στεφάνους.
Κ' εἶχαν συνήθειο πρὸς τὸ τέλος τῆς γιορτῆς
τὰ παλαιά τους ἔθιμα νὰ διηγοῦνται,
καὶ τὰ ἑλληνικὰ ὀνόματα νὰ ξαναλένε,
ποὺ μόλις πιὰ τὰ καταλάμβαναν ὀλίγοι.
Καὶ πάντα μελαγχολικὰ τελείων' ἡ γιορτή τους.
Γιατὶ θυμοῦνταν ποὺ κι αὐτοὶ ἦσαν Ἕλληνες —
Ἰταλιῶται ἕναν καιρὸ κι αὐτοί·
καὶ τώρα πῶς ἐξέπεσαν, πῶς ἔγιναν,
νὰ ζοῦν καὶ νὰ ὁμιλοῦν βαρβαρικὰ
βγαλμένοι — ὦ συμφορά! — ἀπ' τὸν ἑλληνισμό.

1906

[We behave like] the Poseidonians in the Tyrrhenian Gulf, who,
although of Greek origin, became barbarized as Tyrrhenians or
Romans and changed their speech and the customs of their
ancestors. But they observe one Greek festival even to this day;
during this they gather together and call up from memory their
ancient names and customs, and then, lamenting loudly
to each other and weeping, they go away.

    Athenaeus, *Deipnosophistai*, Book 14, 31A (632)

The Poseidonians had forgotten the Greek language
after so many centuries of mingling
with Tyrrhenians, Latins, and other foreigners.
The only thing ancestral that remained to them
was a Greek festival, with beautiful rites,
with lyres and flutes, contests and crowns.
And it was their habit towards the festival's end
to tell each other about their ancient customs
and once again to speak the Greek words
that hardly any of them still understood.
And so their festival always had a melancholy ending
because they remembered that they too were Greeks—
they too citizens of Magna Graecia once upon a time;
but how they'd fallen, what they'd now become,
living and speaking like barbarians,
excluded—what a catastrophe!—from the Hellenic way of life.

ΤΟ ΤΕΛΟΣ ΤΟΥ ΑΝΤΩΝΙΟΥ

Ἀλλὰ σὰν ἄκουσε ποὺ ἐκλαῖγαν οἱ γυναῖκες
καὶ γιὰ τὸ χάλι του ποὺ τὸν θρηνοῦσαν,
μὲ ἀνατολίτικες χειρονομίες ἡ κερά,
κ᾽ οἱ δοῦλες μὲ τὰ ἑλληνικὰ τὰ βαρβαρίζοντα,
ἡ ὑπερηφάνεια μὲς στὴν ψυχή του
σηκώθηκεν, ἀηδίασε τὸ ἰταλικό του αἷμα,
καὶ τὸν ἐφάνηκαν ξένα κι ἀδιάφορα
αὐτὰ ποὺ ὡς τότε λάτρευε τυφλὰ —
ὅλ᾽ ἡ παράφορη Ἀλεξανδρινὴ ζωή του —
κ᾽ εἶπε «Νὰ μὴν τὸν κλαῖνε. Δὲν ταιριάζουν τέτοια.
Μὰ νὰ τὸν ἐξυμνοῦνε πρέπει μᾶλλον,
ποὺ ἐστάθηκε μεγάλος ἐξουσιαστής,
κι ἀπέκτησε τόσ᾽ ἀγαθὰ καὶ τόσα.
Καὶ τώρα ἂν ἔπεσε, δὲν πέφτει ταπεινά,
ἀλλὰ Ρωμαῖος ἀπὸ Ρωμαῖο νικημένος».

1907

THE END OF ANTONY

But when he heard the women wailing,
lamenting the miserable state he was in,
with oriental gestures from the lady of the house, ·
and her slaves with their barbarous Greek,
the pride rose up in his soul,
his Italian blood revolted in disgust,
and all the things once so blindly cherished
now seemed alien and dull—
all his reckless Alexandrian life—
and he told them not to wail for him.
That kind of thing was unbecoming.
They should rather sing his praises
for having been so great a ruler,
for having gained such wealth and glory.
And if he'd fallen now, he wasn't falling humbly,
but as a Roman conquered by a Roman.

Ἀπ᾿ ὅσα ἔκαμα κι ἀπ᾿ ὅσα εἶπα
νὰ μὴ ζητήσουνε νὰ βροῦν ποιὸς ἤμουν.
Ἐμπόδιο στέκονταν καὶ μεταμόρφωνε
τὲς πράξεις καὶ τὸν τρόπο τῆς ζωῆς μου.
Ἐμπόδιο στέκονταν καὶ σταματοῦσε με
πολλὲς φορὲς ποὺ πήγαινα νὰ πῶ.
Οἱ πιὸ ἀπαρατήρητές μου πράξεις
καὶ τὰ γραψίματά μου τὰ πιὸ σκεπασμένα —
ἀπὸ ἐκεῖ μονάχα θὰ μὲ νοιώσουν.
Ἀλλὰ ἴσως δὲν ἀξίζει νὰ καταβληθεῖ
τόση φροντὶς καὶ τόσος κόπος νὰ μὲ μάθουν.
Κατόπι — στὴν τελειοτέρα κοινωνία —
κανένας ἄλλος καμωμένος σὰν ἐμένα
βέβαια θὰ φανεῖ κ᾿ ἐλεύθερα θὰ κάμει.

1908

HIDDEN THINGS

From all the things I did and all the things I said
let no one try to find out who I was.
An obstacle was there transforming
the actions and the manner of my life.
An obstacle was often there
to silence me when I began to speak.
From my most unnoticed actions
and my most veiled writing—
from these alone will I be understood.
But maybe it isn't worth so much concern
and so much effort to discover who I really am.
Later, in a more perfect society,
someone else made just like me
is certain to appear and act freely.

ΕΡΩΤΟΣ ΑΚΟΥΣΜΑ

Στοῦ δυνατοῦ ἔρωτος τὸ ἄκουσμα τρέμε καὶ συγκινήσου
σὰν αἰσθητής. Ὅμως, εὐτυχισμένος,
θυμήσου πόσα ἡ φαντασία σου σ' ἔπλασσεν· αὐτὰ
πρῶτα· κ' ἔπειτα τ' ἄλλα — πιὸ μικρὰ — ποὺ στὴν ζωή σου
ἐπέρασες κι ἀπόλαυσες, τ' ἀληθινότερα κι ἁπτά. —
Ἀπὸ τοὺς τέτοιους ἔρωτας δὲν ἤσουν στερημένος.

1911

ON HEARING OF LOVE

On hearing of powerful love, tremble and be moved
like an aesthete. Yet, fortunate as you've been,
remember how many loves your imagination created for you.
These first, and then the others—lesser ones—that in your life
you experienced and enjoyed: the more real, the tangible ones.
Of loves like these you were not deprived.

«ΤΑ Δ' ΑΛΛΑ ΕΝ ΑΔΟΥ ΤΟΙΣ ΚΑΤΩ
ΜΥΘΗΣΟΜΑΙ»

«Τῷόντι», εἶπ' ὁ ἀνθύπατος, κλείοντας τὸ βιβλίο, «αὐτὸς
ὁ στίχος εἶν' ὡραῖος καὶ πολὺ σωστός·
τὸν ἔγραψεν ὁ Σοφοκλῆς βαθιὰ φιλοσοφῶντας.
Πόσα θὰ ποῦμ' ἐκεῖ, πόσα θὰ ποῦμ' ἐκεῖ,
καὶ πόσο θὰ φανοῦμε διαφορετικοί.
Αὐτὰ ποὺ ἐδῶ σὰν ἄγρυπνοι φρουροὶ βαστοῦμε,
πληγὲς καὶ μυστικὰ ποὺ μέσα μας σφαλνοῦμε,
μὲ καθημερινὴ ἀγωνία βαριά,
ἐλεύθερα ἐκεῖ καὶ καθαρὰ θὰ ποῦμε».

«Πρόσθεσε», εἶπε ὁ σοφιστής, μισοχαμογελῶντας,
«ἂν τέτοια λὲν ἐκεῖ, ἂν τοὺς μέλλει πιά».

1913

"Indeed," said the proconsul, closing the book,   *35*
"this line is beautiful and very true.
Sophocles wrote it in a deeply philosophic mood.
How much we will tell down there, how much,
and how very different we will look.
What we protect here like sleepless guards,
wounds and secrets locked inside us,
with an oppressive daily anxiety—
we will reveal freely and clearly down there."

"You might add," said the sophist, half smiling,
"*if* they talk about things like that down there,
if they bother at all about them any more."

ΕΤΣΙ

Στὴν ἄσεμνην αὐτὴ φωτογραφία ποὺ κρυφὰ
στὸν δρόμο (ὁ ἀστυνόμος νὰ μὴ δεῖ) πουλήθηκε,
στὴν πορνικὴν αὐτὴ φωτογραφία
πῶς βρέθηκε τέτοιο ἕνα πρόσωπο
τοῦ ὀνείρου· ἐδῶ πῶς βρέθηκες ἐσύ.

Ποιὸς ξέρει τί ξευτελισμένη, πρόστυχη ζωὴ θὰ ζεῖς·
τί ἀπαίσιο θά 'ταν τὸ περιβάλλον
ὅταν θὰ στάθηκες νὰ σὲ φωτογραφήσουν·
τί ποταπὴ ψυχὴ θὰ εἶν' ἡ δική σου.
Μὰ μ' ὅλα αὐτά, καὶ πιότερα, γιὰ μένα μένεις
τὸ πρόσωπο τοῦ ὀνείρου, ἡ μορφὴ
γιὰ ἑλληνικὴ ἡδονὴ πλασμένη καὶ δοσμένη —
ἔτσι γιὰ μένα μένεις καὶ σὲ λέγ' ἡ ποίησίς μου.

1913

THE PHOTOGRAPH

In this obscene photograph secretly sold
(the policeman mustn't see) around the corner,
in this whorish photograph,
how did such a dream-like face
make its way? How did you get in here?

Who knows what a degrading, vulgar life you lead;
how horrible the surroundings must have been
when you posed to have the picture taken;
what a cheap soul you must have.
But in spite of all this, and even more, you remain for me
the dream-like face, the figure
shaped for and dedicated to Hellenic love—
that's how you remain for me
and how my poetry speaks of you.

ΕΠΑΝΟΔΟΣ ΑΠΟ ΤΗΝ ΕΛΛΑΔΑ

῟Ωστε κοντεύουμε νὰ φθάσουμ', ῞Ερμιππε.
Μεθαύριο, θαρρῶ· ἔτσ' εἶπε ὁ πλοίαρχος.
Τουλάχιστον στὴν θάλασσά μας πλέουμε·
νερὰ τῆς Κύπρου, τῆς Συρίας, καὶ τῆς Αἰγύπτου,
ἀγαπημένα τῶν πατρίδων μας νερά.
Γιατί ἔτσι σιωπηλός; Ρώτησε τὴν καρδιά σου,
ὅσο ποὺ ἀπ' τὴν ῾Ελλάδα μακρυνόμεθαν
δὲν χαίροσουν καὶ σύ; ᾿Αξίζει νὰ γελιούμαστε; —
αὐτὸ δὲν θά 'ταν βέβαια ἑλληνοπρεπές.

῎Ας τὴν παραδεχθοῦμε τὴν ἀλήθεια πιά·
εἴμεθα ῞Ελληνες κ' ἐμεῖς — τί ἄλλο εἴμεθα; —
ἀλλὰ μὲ ἀγάπες καὶ μὲ συγκινήσεις τῆς ᾿Ασίας,
ἀλλὰ μὲ ἀγάπες καὶ μὲ συγκινήσεις
ποὺ κάποτε ξενίζουν τὸν ἑλληνισμό.

Δὲν μᾶς ταιριάζει, ῞Ερμιππε, ἐμᾶς τοὺς φιλοσόφους
νὰ μοιάζουμε σὰν κάτι μικροβασιλεῖς μας
(θυμᾶσαι πῶς γελούσαμε μὲ δαύτους
σὰν ἐπισκέπτονταν τὰ σπουδαστήριά μας)
ποὺ κάτω ἀπ' τὸ ἐξωτερικό τους τὸ ἐπιδεικτικὰ
ἑλληνοποιημένο, καὶ (τί λόγος!) μακεδονικό,
καμιὰ ᾿Αραβία ξεμυτίζει κάθε τόσο

RETURN FROM GREECE

Well, we're nearly there, Hermippus.
Day after tomorrow, it seems. So the captain said.
At least we're sailing in our seas,
the waters of Cyprus, of Syria and Egypt,
cherished waters of our native lands.
Why so silent? Ask your heart:
as we left Greece behind
weren't you just as glad as I was?
Is it worth fooling ourselves?
That would certainly be unhellenic.

It's time we faced the truth:
we too are Greeks—what else are we?—
but with the affections and emotions of Asia,
with affections and emotions
that hellenism sometimes finds strange.

It isn't fitting, Hermippus, for us philosophers
to let ourselves resemble certain of our minor kings
(remember how we laughed at them
when they came to visit our lecture halls?)
who under their showy hellenified exteriors
(and—it goes without saying—Macedonian)
let a bit of Arabia show through every now and then,

καμιὰ Μηδία ποὺ δὲν περιμαζεύεται,
καὶ μὲ τί κωμικὰ τεχνάσματα οἱ καϋμένοι
πασχίζουν νὰ μὴ παρατηρηθεῖ.

Ἄ, ὄχι, δὲν ταιριάζουνε σ᾽ ἐμᾶς αὐτά.
Σ᾽ Ἕλληνας σὰν κ᾽ ἐμᾶς δὲν κάνουν τέτοιες μικροπρέπειες.
Τὸ αἷμα τῆς Συρίας καὶ τῆς Αἰγύπτου
ποὺ ῥέει μὲς στὲς φλέϐες μας νὰ μὴ ντραπούμε,
νὰ τὸ τιμήσουμε καὶ νὰ τὸ καυχηθούμε.

1914

a bit of Media too slippery to control;
and with what comic artifice the poor fools
exert themselves to make it pass unnoticed.

No, that kind of thing doesn't suit us at all.
For Greeks like us such pettiness won't do.
The blood of Syria and Egypt
that runs in our veins is nothing to be ashamed of:
let us honor it, let us boast about it.

ΦΥΓΑΔΕΣ

Πάντα ἡ ᾽Αλεξάνδρεια εἶναι. Λίγο νὰ βαδίσεις
στὴν ἴσια της ὁδὸ ποὺ στὸ Ἱπποδρόμιο παύει,
θὰ δεῖς παλάτια καὶ μνημεῖα ποὺ θ᾽ ἀπορήσεις.
῍Οσο κι ἂν ἔπαθεν ἀπ᾽ τοὺς πολέμους βλάβη
ὅσο κι ἂν μίκραινε, πάντα θαυμάσια χώρα.
Κ᾽ ἔπειτα μ᾽ ἐκδρομές, καὶ μὲ βιβλία,
καὶ μὲ σπουδὲς διάφορες περνᾶ ἡ ὥρα.
Τὸ βράδυ μαζευόμεθα στὴν παραλία
ἡμεῖς οἱ πέντε (μὲ ὀνόματα ὅλοι
πλαστὰ βεβαίως) κι ἄλλοι μερικοὶ Γραικοὶ
ἀπ᾽ τοὺς ὀλίγους ὅπου μείνανε στὴν πόλι.
Πότε μιλοῦμε γιὰ ἐκκλησιαστικὰ (κάπως λατινικοὶ
μοιάζουν ἐδῶ), πότε φιλολογία.
Προχθὲς τοῦ Νόννου στίχους ἐδιαβάζαμε.
Τί εἰκόνες, τί ρυθμός, τί γλῶσσα, τί ἁρμονία.
᾽Ενθουσιασμένοι τὸν Πανοπολίτην ἐθαυμάζαμε.
῍Ετσι περνοῦν οἱ μέρες, κ᾽ ἡ διαμονὴ
δυσάρεστη δὲν εἶναι, γιατὶ, ἐννοεῖται,
δὲν πρόκειται νά᾽ναι παντοτεινή.
Καλὲς εἰδήσεις λάβαμε, καὶ εἴτε
ἀπὸ τὴν Σμύρνη κάτι γίνει τώρα, εἴτε τὸν ᾽Απρίλιο
οἱ φίλοι μας κινήσουν ἀπ᾽ τὴν ῍Ηπειρο, τὰ σχέδιά μας
ἐπιτυγχάνουν, καὶ τὸν ρίχνουμεν εὐκόλως τὸν Βασίλειο.
Καὶ τότε πιὰ κ᾽ ἐμᾶς θά᾽ρθ᾽ ἡ σειρά μας.

1914

EXILES

It goes on being Alexandria still. If you take a walk
along its straight road ending at the Hippodrome,
you will see palaces and monuments that will amaze you.
Whatever damage it may have suffered from the wars,
however much smaller it's become,
it goes on being a wonderful city.
Besides, with excursions, and books,
and studying of various kinds, time passes.
In the evenings we gather on the seashore
we five (all of us naturally
under fictitious names) and some other Greeks
of the few still remaining in the city.
Sometimes we discuss church affairs (they seem
a bit Popish here), sometimes literature.
The other day we read through some lines by Nonnos.
What imagery, what rhythm, what diction, what harmony.
Excited, we gave the Panopolitan all our admiration.
So the days go by, and our stay here
is not unpleasant because naturally
it's not going to go on forever.
We've received good news, and whether
something is going to happen now in Smyrna, or whether
our friends from Epiros decide to move in April, our plans
are bound to succeed, and we can easily overthrow Basil.
And then at last our turn will come.

ΘΕΟΦΙΛΟΣ ΠΑΛΑΙΟΛΟΓΟΣ

Ὁ τελευταῖος χρόνος εἶν' αὐτός. Ὁ τελευταῖος τῶν Γραικῶν
αὐτοκρατόρων εἶν' αὐτός. Κι ἀλλοίμονον
τί θλιβερὰ ποὺ ὁμιλοῦν πλησίον του.
Ἐν τῇ ἀπογνώσει του, ἐν τῇ ὀδύνῃ,
ὁ Κὺρ Θεόφιλος Παλαιολόγος
λέγει «Θέλω θανεῖν μᾶλλον ἢ ζῆν».

Ἄ, Κὺρ Θεόφιλε Παλαιολόγο,
πόσον καϋμὸ τοῦ γένους μας, καὶ πόση ἐξάντλησι
(πόσην ἀπηύδησιν ἀπὸ ἀδικίες καὶ κατατρεγμὸ)
οἱ τραγικές σου πέντε λέξεις περιεῖχαν.

1914

THEOPHILOS PALAIOLOGOS

This is the last year. This is the last
of the Greek emperors. And, alas,
how sadly those around him talk.
Kyr Theophilos Palaiologos
in his grief, in his despair, says:
"I would rather die than live."

Ah, Kyr Theophilos Palaiologos,
how much of the sorrow, the regret of our race
how much weariness (surfeit of injustice and persecution)
your six tragic words contained.

ΚΙ ΑΚΟΥΜΠΗΣΑ ΚΑΙ ΠΛΑΓΙΑΣΑ ΣΤΕΣ ΚΛΙΝΕΣ ΤΩΝ

Στῆς ἡδονῆς τὸ σπίτι ὅταν μπῆκα,
δὲν ἔμεινα στὴν αἴθουσαν ὅπου γιορτάζουν
μὲ κάποια τάξιν ἀναγνωρισμένοι ἔρωτες.

Στὲς κάμαρες ἐπῆγα τὲς κρυφὲς
κι ἀκούμπησα καὶ πλάγιασα στὲς κλίνες των.

Στὲς κάμαρες ἐπῆγα τὲς κρυφὲς
ποὺ τό'χουν γιὰ ντροπὴ καὶ νὰ τὲς ὀνομάσουν.
Μὰ ὄχι ντροπὴ γιὰ μένα — γιατὶ τότε
τί ποιητὴς καὶ τί τεχνίτης θά'μουν;
Καλλίτερα ν' ἀσκήτευα. Θά'ταν πιὸ σύμφωνο,
πολὺ πιὸ σύμφωνο μὲ τὴν ποίησί μου·
παρὰ μὲς στὴν κοινότοπην αἴθουσα νὰ χαρῶ.

1915

AND I LEANED AND LAY ON THEIR BEDS

When I went into the house of pleasure
I didn't stay in the lounge where they celebrate,
with some decorum, the accepted modes of love.

I went into the secret rooms
and leaned and lay on their beds.

I went into the secret rooms
considered shameful even to name.
But not shameful to me—because then
what kind of poet, what kind of artist would I be?
I'd rather be an ascetic. That would be more fitting,
much more fitting with my poetry,
than for me to find pleasure in the commonplace lounge.

ΜΙΣΗ ΩΡΑ

Μήτε σὲ ἀπέκτησα, μήτε θασὲ ἀποκτήσω
ποτέ, θαρρῶ. Μερικὰ λόγια, ἕνα πλησίασμα
ὅπως στὸ μπὰρ προχθές, καὶ τίποτε ἄλλο.
Εἶναι, δὲν λέγω, λύπη. Ἀλλὰ ἐμεῖς τῆς Τέχνης,
κάποτε μ' ἔντασι τοῦ νοῦ, καὶ βέβαια μόνο
γιὰ λίγην ὥρα, δημιουργοῦμεν ἡδονὴν
ἡ ὁποία σχεδὸν σὰν ὑλικὴ φαντάζει.
Ἔτσι στὸ μπὰρ προχθὲς — βοηθῶντας κιόλας
πολὺ ὁ εὐσπλαχνικὸς ἀλκολισμὸς —
εἶχα μισὴ ὥρα τέλεια ἐρωτική.
Καὶ τὸ κατάλαβες μὲ φαίνεται,
κ' ἔμεινες κάτι περισσότερον ἐπίτηδες.
Ἦταν πολλὴ ἀνάγκη αὐτό. Γιατὶ
μ' ὅλην τὴν φαντασία, καὶ μὲ τὸ μάγο οἰνόπνευμα,
χρειάζονταν νὰ βλέπω καὶ τὰ χείλη σου,
χρειάζονταν νά'ναι τὸ σῶμα σου κοντά.

1917

HALF AN HOUR

I never had you, nor will I ever have you,
I suppose. A few words, an approach,
as in the bar yesterday, and nothing more.
It's regretful, I admit. But we who serve Art,
sometimes by intensity of mind and of course only
for a short time, are able to create pleasure
which seems almost tangible.
That's how in the bar yesterday—
with the help of compassionate alcohol—
I had half an hour that was totally erotic.
And I think you understood this
and stayed a little longer on purpose.
It was very necessary, that. Because
for all the imagination, for all the magic alcohol,
I needed to see your lips as well,
I needed your body to be near.

Τὰ ξέρω, ναί, τὰ νέα ποιήματά του·
ἐνθουσιάσθηκεν ἡ Βηρυτὸς μ' αὐτά.
Μιὰν ἄλλη μέρα θὰ τὰ μελετήσω.
Σήμερα δὲν μπορῶ, γιατ' εἶμαι κάπως ταραγμένος.

'Απ' τὸν Λιβάνιο πιὸ ἑλληνομαθὴς εἶναι βεβαίως.
"Ομως καλλίτερος κι ἀπ' τὸν Μελέαγρο; Δὲν πιστεύω.

῎Α, Μέβη, τί Λιβάνιος! καὶ τί βιβλία!
καὶ τί μικρότητες!..... Μέβη, ἤμουν χθὲς —
ἡ τύχη τό'φερε — κάτω ἀπ' τοῦ Συμεὼν τὸν στύλο.

Χώθηκα ἀνάμεσα στοὺς Χριστιανοὺς
ποὺ σιωπηλοὶ προσεύχονταν κ' ἐλάτρευαν,
καὶ προσκυνοῦσαν· πλὴν μὴ ὄντας Χριστιανὸς
τὴν ψυχικὴ γαλήνη των δὲν εἶχα —
κ' ἔτρεμα ὁλόκληρος καὶ ὑπόφερνα·
κ' ἔφριττα, καὶ ταράττομουν, καὶ παθαινόμουν.

῎Α, μὴ χαμογελᾶς· τριάντα πέντε χρόνια, σκέψου —
χειμῶνα, καλοκαῖρι, νύχτα, μέρα, τριάντα πέντε
χρόνια ἐπάνω σ' ἕναν στύλο ζεῖ καὶ μαρτυρεῖ.
Πρὶν γεννηθοῦμ' ἐμεῖς — ἐγὼ εἶμαι εἴκοσι ἐνιὰ ἐτῶν,
ἐσὺ θαρρῶ εἶσαι νεότερός μου —

SIMEON

Yes, I know his new poems;
all Beirut is raving about them.
I'll study them some other day.
I can't today because I'm rather upset.

Certainly he's more learned in Greek than Libanius.
But a better poet than Meleager? I don't think so.

O Mebis, no more of Libanius and books
and all these trivialities. Mebis, yesterday
(it happened by chance) I found myself under Simeon's pillar.

I slipped in among the Christians
who were praying and worshipping in silence,
on their knees; not being a Christian myself
I couldn't share their spiritual peace—
I trembled all over and suffered;
I shuddered, disturbed and completely involved.

Please don't smile; for thirty-five years—think of it—
winter and summer, night and day, for thirty-five years
he's been living and suffering on top of a pillar.
Before either of us was born (I'm twenty-nine,
you must be younger than me),

πρὶν γεννηθοῦμ' ἐμεῖς, φαντάσου το,
ἀνέβηκεν ὁ Συμεὼν στὸν στύλο
κ' ἔκτοτε μένει αὐτοῦ ἐμπρὸς εἰς τὸν Θεό.

Δὲν ἔχω σήμερα κεφάλι γιὰ δουλειά. —
Πλὴν τοῦτο, Μέβη, κάλλιο νὰ τὸ πεῖς:
ποὺ ὅ,τι κι ἂν λὲν οἱ ἄλλοι σοφισταί,
ἐγὼ τὸν παραδέχομαι τὸν Λάμονα
γιὰ πρῶτο τῆς Συρίας ποιητή.

1917

before we were born, just imagine,
Simeon climbed up his pillar
and has stayed there ever since facing God.

I have no mind for work today—
but Mebis, I think it better that you tell them this:
whatever the other sophists may say,
I at least recognize Lamon
as Syria's greatest poet.

Ο ΔΕΜΕΝΟΣ ΩΜΟΣ

Εἶπε ποὺ χτύπησε σὲ τοῖχον ἢ ποὺ ἔπεσε.
Μὰ πιθανὸν ἡ αἰτία νά᾽ταν ἄλλη
τοῦ πληγωμένου καὶ δεμένου ὤμου.

Μὲ μιὰ κομμάτι βίαιη κίνησιν,
ἀπ᾽ ἕνα ράφι γιὰ νὰ κατεβάσει κάτι
φωτογραφίες ποὺ ἤθελε νὰ δεῖ ἀπὸ κοντά,
λύθηκεν ὁ ἐπίδεσμος κ᾽ ἔτρεξε λίγο αἷμα.

Ξανάδεσα τὸν ὦμο, καὶ στὸ δέσιμο
ἀργοῦσα κάπως· γιατὶ δὲν πονοῦσε,
καὶ μ᾽ ἄρεζε νὰ βλέπω τὸ αἷμα. Πρᾶγμα
τοῦ ἔρωτός μου τὸ αἷμα ἐκεῖνο ἦταν.

Σὰν ἔφυγε ηὗρα στὴν καρέγλα ἐμπρός,
ἕνα κουρέλι ματωμένο, ἀπ᾽ τὰ πανιά,
κουρέλι ποὺ ἔμοιαζε γιὰ τὰ σκουπίδια κατ᾽ εὐθείαν·
καὶ ποὺ στὰ χείλη μου τὸ πῆρα ἐγώ,
καὶ ποὺ τὸ φύλαξα ὥρα πολλὴ —
τὸ αἷμα τοῦ ἔρωτος στὰ χείλη μου ἐπάνω.

1919

THE BANDAGED SHOULDER

He said he'd hurt himself against a wall or had fallen down.   55
But there was probably some other reason
for the wounded, the bandaged shoulder.

With a rather abrupt gesture,
reaching for a shelf to bring down
some photographs he wanted to examine,
the bandage came undone and a little blood showed.

I did it up again, taking my time
over the binding; he wasn't in pain
and I liked looking at the blood.
It was a thing of my love, that blood.

When he left, I found, in front of his chair,
a bloody rag, part of the dressing,
a rag to be thrown straight into the garbage;
I put it to my lips
and kept it there a long while—
the blood of love against my lips.

NOTES

1. From a note found among Cavafy's papers and dated 1906. The full text, which Cavafy wrote in English, appears in G. P. Savidis, *The Editions of Cavafy (1891–1932)* (Athens, 1966), p. 107.

2. Cavafy began writing at least as early as 1882, mainly in Greek, but also in English and French. He published three of these early poems in a Leipzig periodical during 1886. Most of the remaining poems were mercilessly destroyed or drastically revised in 1891. That year was the starting point in his mind, but only a starting point, because after a long series of poetic liquidations, revisions, and "philosophical scrutinies" (see the so-called *Ars Poetica* by Cavafy that appeared in *The Charioteer*, No. 10, New York, 1968, p. 72), the poet located the beginning of his creative maturity at the age of forty-eight by dividing his œuvre into those poems written before 1911 and those he went on writing until 1932, the year before his death from cancer on April 29, 1933 (his seventieth birthday). Of the six poems published between 1891 and 1904, three were never allowed to appear in print again. These, and some twenty others that came out in ephemeral publications, constitute the rejected portion of his published work, included among the "Early Poems" in *The Complete Poems of Cavafy*, trans. Rae Dalven (New York, 1961).

3. These twenty-one poems, plus "Walls" (1897), "The City" (1910), and "The Satrapy" (1910), form that part of his acknowledged corpus which Cavafy chose to designate as pre-1911 (see fn. 2 above).

4. The booklets included the initial ten poems first published in 1910–1911, plus two poems dated 1909 and drawn from the 1910 pamplet, the twelve poems rearranged thematically.

5. The first booklet contained forty poems first published between 1905 and 1915, and the second contained twenty-eight poems

published between 1916 and 1918. The folder held poems published in broadsheet form after 1918.

6. This edition included 153 poems previously printed by Cavafy, plus the last poem he wrote ("On the Outskirts of Antioch"): what has been the accepted canon of Cavafy's poetry since 1935 and what we refer to here as the "collected" poems, first translated into English by John Mavrogordato and published as *The Poems of C. P. Cavafy* (London, 1951).

7. See C. P. Cavafy, *Unpublished Poems, 1882–1923*, ed. G. P. Savidis, published by the firm of Ikaros (Athens, 1968).

8. *Ibid.*

9. See G. P. Savidis, *The Editions of Cavafy*, op. cit., p. 209.

10. "Passions" and "Ancient Days" were among the titles that Cavafy used in filing and grouping his poems.

11. For the English titles of the collected poems, we have used those which appear in the first English translation of the collected edition, *The Poems of C. P. Cavafy*, op. cit.. In this instance, the table of contents (as distinct from the text) designates the title as "Julian and the Men of Antioch."

12. See the following unpublished poems not included in this selection: "The Afterlife" (1892), "In the Cemetery" (1893), and "Fear" (1894).

13. *Two Cheers for Democracy* (London, 1951), pp. 249–250.

14. In his introduction to *The Complete Poems of Cavafy*, op. cit..

The source of this poem, originally titled "Julian at Eleusis," is almost certainly the following passage from Gibbon's *Decline and Fall* (Ch. XXIII):

> His residence at Athens [c. 354 A.D.] confirmed this unnatural alliance of philosophy and superstition. He obtained the privilege of a solemn initiation into the mysteries of Eleusis, which, amidst the general decay of the Grecian worship, still retained some vestiges of their primaeval sanctity; . . . As these ceremonies were performed in the depths of caverns, and in the silence of the night; and as the inviolable secret of the mysteries was preserved by the discretion of the initiated, I shall not presume to describe the horrid sounds, and fiery apparitions, which were presented to the senses, or the imagination, of the credulous aspirant . . .

Equally relevant is Gibbon's note at this point:

> When Julian, in a momentary panic, made the sign of the cross, the daemons instantly disappeared (Greg. Naz. Orat. iii, p. 71). Gregory supposes that they were frightened, but the priest declared that they were indignant. The reader, according to the measure of his faith, will determine this profound question.

The "Bishop of Nicomedia" mentioned in line 21 was Julian's spiritual tutor. According to Gibbon, the care of Julian's infancy "was entrusted to Eusebius, bishop of Nicomedia, who was related to him on the side of his mother; and till Julian reached the twentieth year of his age [i.e., 351 A.D.], he received from his Christian preceptors the education not of a hero, but of a saint."

The poem was written in November, 1896. It was originally classed with five other poems, now lost, under the heading "The Beginnings of Christianity." Along with "Julian and the Citizens of Antioch," among the collected poems, compare the following: "Julian Seeing Negligence" (1923), "Julian in Nicomedia" (1924), "A Great Procession of Priests and Laymen" (1926), "Understood Not" (1928), and "On the Outskirts of Antioch" (1933).

KING CLAUDIUS

The poem was written in July, 1899. There is a tag, in English, attached to the manuscript: "Not for publication; but may remain here [i.e., among Cavafy's papers]." It is the longest extant poem by the poet. Cavafy seems to have written another poem inspired by *Hamlet* in October, 1899, but only the title, "The State of Denmark," has survived.

WHEN THE WATCHMAN SAW THE LIGHT

The poem was written in January, 1900. It derives directly from the prologue of Aeschylus' *Agamemnon*. Three months earlier, Cavafy wrote another poem inspired by Aeschylus' *Persians*, under the title "The Naval Battle," and this too remained unpublished during his lifetime. Aeschylus appears among the collected poems in the epigraph to "Treachery" (1904) and in "Young Men of Sidon" (1920).

The original is in rhymed couplets.

STRENGTHENING THE SPIRIT

The poem was probably written in June, 1903. There is a tag on the manuscript (in Greek): "Not for publication; but may remain here." The title literally means "invigoration."

The original is loosely rhymed.

According to a note by Cavafy, this poem and the one that follows it
"were really written in October and December 1903, but were perfected
and catalogued in January 1904." The manuscript was found in
the file titled "Passions," and it bears the initials "A. M.", which
almost certainly refer to a minor Athenian poet of those years, Aleco
Mavroudis, who later moved to Paris, where he won an ephemeral
reputation as a fashionable playwright under the pen name Alex Madis.
Cavafy probably met him during his second visit to Athens, from
August to October of 1903.

The following comment on the two "A. M." poems appears among
Cavafy's *Unpublished Prose Texts*, ed. M. Peridis (Athens, 1963), pp. 54
ff. (the original in English):

25 November 1903

. . . No poems were sincerer than the "2 M[onth]s," written during and
immediately after the great cr[isis] of lib[eration] succeeding on my departure
from Athens. Now, say that in time Ale. Mav. comes to be indifferent to me,
like Sul. (I was very much in love with h[im] before my departure for
Athens), or Bra.; will the poems—so true when they were made—become
false? Certainly, certainly not. They will remain true in the past, and, though
not applicable any more in my life, seeing that they may remind of a day and
perhaps different impression, they will be applicable to feelings of other lives.

The same therefore must apply to other works—really felt at the time. If
even for one day, or one hour I felt like the man within "Walls," or like the
man of "Windows," the poem is based on a truth, a short-lived truth, but
which, for the very reason of its having once existed, may repeat itself in
another life, perhaps with as short duration, perhaps with longer. If
"Thermopylae" fits but one life, it is true; and it may, indeed the
probabilities are that it must.

See the previous note, and c.f. "Days of 1903" (1917) among the
collected poems.

ON THE STAIRS

The poem was written in February, 1904. The manuscript, included in
the "Passions" file, carries the English inscription "Unknown,"
presumably referring to the character described in the poem.

AT THE THEATRE

The poem was written in March, 1904. The manuscript, also in the
"Passions" file, shows the initial "S".

POSEIDONIANS

Poseidonia, near the modern town of Salerno, is better known under its
Roman name, Paestum. As a Greek colony, it was founded after
600 B.C. and flourished until 438 B.C. The custom mentioned by
Athenaeus (fl. c. 200 A.D.) probably dates from the end of the fourth
century B.C. In 273 B.C., Poseidonia became a Roman garrison and
changed its name.

The poem was written in August, 1906, and the manuscript carries
the English tag: "Not for publication, but may remain here." The
epigraph reveals a number of omissions and alterations; if it wasn't
taken from a faulty secondary source, we can assume that Cavafy
quoted it from memory.

THE END OF ANTONY

Along with the most famous poems from the 31 B.C. cycle, "The God
Abandons Antony" and "Alexandrian Kings," see "Kaisarion" (1918),

"In Alexandria, 31 B.C." (1924), and "In a Township of Asia Minor" (1926).

The poem was written in June, 1907, and the manuscript carries the following shorthand note in English: "Too sti[lted?] howe[ver]."

HIDDEN THINGS

The poem was written in April, 1908.

ON HEARING OF LOVE

The poem was written in June, 1911. The manuscript, included in the "Passions" file, carries the date "7 April 1910," which is somewhat clarified by a note (in Greek): "The hearing was in the summer of 1910. Those things about E. M."

The original is rhymed a,b,c,a,c,b.

"THE REST I WILL TELL TO THOSE DOWN IN HADES"

The poem was first written in November, 1893, and then rewritten in February, 1913. The title is a quotation from Sophocles' *Ajax* (i.e., Ajax's last words before his suicide).

The original is rhymed a,a,b,c,c,d,d,e,d,b,e.

THE PHOTOGRAPH

The poem was written in April, 1913, and the manuscript was found in the "Passions" file. The title in the original means "so" or "thus."

RETURN FROM GREECE

The poem was written in July, 1914. In addition to "A Prince from Western Libya," among the collected poems, c.f. "Philhellene" (1912).

The anonymous exiles of the poem cannot be identified precisely, yet their situation falls well within historical possibility. The scene is set in Alexandria after its conquest by the Arabs (642) and probably shortly after the murder of the Byzantine Emperor Michael III by his co-emperor Basil I (867–886), founder of the Macedonian dynasty. The mention of "latinized" (possibly "latin-minded") Christians further points to the period of the Photian schism (867–870), when its initiator, the Patriarch of Constantinople, Photius, had been deposed by the Emperor and most of his friends had been driven into exile. The "Panopolitan" of line 17 is of course the Egyptian-Greek epic poet Nonnus (fl. c. 400 A.D.) mentioned in line 15.

The poem was written in October, 1914. A related theme is treated in the collected poem "A Byzantine Nobleman in Exile" (1921).

The original is rhymed a,b,a,b,c,d,c,d, etc..

THEOPHILOS PALAIOLOGOS

Theophilos Palaiologos was a kinsman of Constantine Palaiologos, the last emperor of Byzantium. Grammarian, humanist, and mathematician, he was given command of the troops defending the sector of the Gate of Silyvria during the last siege of Constantinople by the Turks in 1453, and was killed during the final desperate battle, fighting gallantly at the side of his Emperor.

The date of the first version of the poem, listed under the heading "Byzantine Days," is unknown. We do know that in March, 1903, Cavafy rewrote a poem entitled "I Would Rather Die Than Live." The extant version is undated but certainly later. Since the manuscript is accompanied by relevant quotes from, and references to, books published in 1914, we have tentatively dated the poem in that year.

AND I LEANED AND LAY ON THEIR BEDS

The poem was written in September, 1915, and the manuscript was
included in the "Passions" file.

HALF AN HOUR

The poem was written in January, 1917, and was also included among
the "Passions."

SIMEON

The anonymous speaker and his listener (Mebis) are very probably fictitious characters. The poet places them in Syria around 454 A.D., that is,
thirty-five years after Simeon Stylites the Elder ascended his pillar and
five years before his death. The other historical characters mentioned
are Libanius (c. 314–393 A.D.), the Syrian rhetorician who taught Julian
and St. John Chrysostom, and Meleager (fl. c. 60 B.C.), who has been
described as "a Greek poet of exquisite ability within his limited sphere
. . . and the compiler of an early anthology of epigrams" (*Oxford
Companion to Classical Literature*). The poet Lamon, who serves as a
pretext for the poem, is also probably a fictitious character; in choosing
the name, the poet may have had in mind the scholarly joke: "In the
lands of the blind, Lamon reigns." Cavafy's early preoccupation with
Simeon as an important poetical theme can be discerned from the
following marginal note in his hand, written about 1899 and inserted in
his copy of Gibbon (Ch. XXXVII) [first published by M. Peridis, *op.
cit.*, pp. 70 ff.]:

> This great, this wonderful saint is surely an object to be singled out in ec-
> clesiastical history for admiration and study. He has been, perhaps, the only
> man who has dared to be really *alone*.

There is no exaggeration in the words "Simeon was repeatedly saved from pious suicide." To make the sense clearer the word *unintentional* should be added. St. Blasius once saved Simeon when he was on the point of expiring from suffering.

The height of the column is correctly given by Gibbon [i.e., sixty feet]. There is an extant passage of Evagrius in which it is stated that Simeon Stylites built a small house, or rather a small room, on the top of the column. But a modern German savant, Gregorovius, is of opinion [sic] that Simeon must have used the room only during the first years till he got used to the vertiginous height, and must afterwards have pulled it down.

The glory of Simeon filled and astounded the earth. Innumerable pilgrims crowded round his column. People came from the farthest West and from the farthest East, from Britain and from India, to gaze on the unique sight—on this candle of faith (such is the magnificent language of the historian Theodoret) set up and lit on a lofty chandelier.

I have met with only one poem on Simeon Stylites, but it is in no way worthy of the subject.

The poem of Tennyson, though it contains some well-made verses, fails in tone. Its great defect lies in its form of a monologue. The complaints of Simeon, his eagerness for the "meed of saints, the white robe and the palm," his dubious humility, his latent vanity, are not objectionable in themselves and may be [sic] were necessary to the poem, but they have been handled in a common, almost a vulgar manner. It was a very difficult task—a task reserved, perhaps, for some mighty king of art—to find fitting language for so great a saint, so wonderful a man.

C.

The poem was written in July, 1917.

THE BANDAGED SHOULDER

The poem was written in May, 1919, and included in the "Passions" file.